Birmingham F

on old picture postcards

John Marks

SNOW HILL STATION BIRMINGHAM.   BOOKING HALL.   DEC 1912.   F.f.&.b.

1. The interior of the booking hall at **Snow Hill** station immediately after its reconstruction in 1912. The area under the clock was a favourite meeting place for fifty years.

£3.50

INTRODUCTION

The Railway came to Birmingham, firstly from Liverpool in 1837 and secondly from London in 1838 but not to the city centre. Curzon Street and then Lawley Street, were the first termini. These were not convenient for travellers or for goods from the other side of the city and the time taken from the termini to the city centre was disproportionate to the length of the journey to Birmingham. Consequently New Street and Snow Hill were developed to meet the demand.

Railway travel initially was only envisaged for long distances, much as our inter-city trains run today. Commuter services were not considered, so that virtually no suburban stations were built. However, it was soon realised that large numbers of workers could be moved quickly over relatively short distances, and additional stations were opened. This helped to pave the way for urbanising villages round Birmingham. Indeed, towards the end of the 19th century, lines purely for suburban use, such as 'The Birmingham West Suburban', were built. By 1900, except for the North Warwickshire Line, the railway network within Birmingham had reached its maximum coverage.

Picture postcards, first published in Britain in 1894, became most popular in the 1902-14 period, and railway subjects were extensively covered. It is possible, for instance, to locate cards featuring the majority of stations in the Birmingham area at a time when they were a focal point for local communities. Local publishers such as Frank Nightingale and George E. Lewis are among those represented in this book. After the first world war, more privately-produced cards by railway enthusiasts emerged.

The illustrations chosen represent a selection of postcards designed to give a flavour of the Birmingham railway system in the first few decades of this century.

John Marks
March 1993

ISBN 0 946245 73 8

Back cover (top): Handsworth Wood station, on the line between Perry Barr and Smethwick, a 'loop' around the northern suburbs of Birmingham between 1896 and 1941. This fine photographic card shows a c.1910 scene, and a large number of passengers having alighted from the departing train.

(bottom): Tyseley Junction about 1920. To the right is the North Warwickshire line to Stratford-on-Avon, to the left the Leamington-Oxford-London Paddington G.W.R. route.

2. The first railway into Birmingham was the Grand Junction, between Birmingham and Liverpool, opened in 1837, followed by the Birmingham and London in 1838. Both lines used Curzon Street as the terminus.

3. Both these cards are officials published by the London and North Western Railway Company in 1905, reproducing contemporary engravings of the station.

4. New Street station and Queens Hotel were designed by William Livock and opened in 1854 for the London, Birmingham and Grand Junction lines. Official L.N.W.R. card, posted in January 1905.

5. This somewhat fanciful impression of the hotel shows the enlargement of 1911 with the front filled in, tower-like projections, and additional floors. All were demolished in the 1960s. Another L.N.W.R. card.

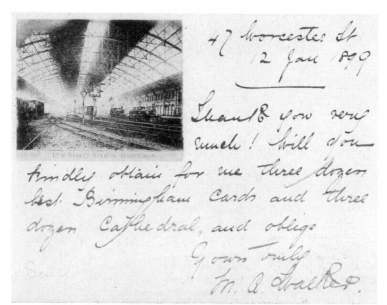

6. This is a very early postcard, sent from Birmingham in January 1899. It has a vignette version of the view of New Street station shown on the card below.

7. Postcard published by Scott Russell & Co. and postally used in April 1905. *"Shall not be able to come with you this afternoon,"* wrote the sender confidently to a friend in Bristol Street. The postmark gives a 1 p.m. cancellation time.

The glass and iron roof of the station was 1,100 ft. long, 212 ft. wide, and 80 ft. high. It was damaged by bombing and taken down in 1945.

8. Initially, seven acres of slum property were cleared to build the station. In 1852 a temporary platform was opened to take the Birmingham-Wolverhampton-Stour Valley Railway. Card published by Henry Wood of Birmingham in the 'City Real Photo' series,

and posted at Acocks Green in April 1906. The South Coast Express to Brighton and Eastbourne is waiting to leave. This train departed New Street at 1 p.m. and arrived at Eastbourne five hours later.

9. By 1854 the station, as planned at that time, was completed to take the London-Manchester-Liverpool and Midland Railway lines. 'Adco' series card published by Adams & Co. from a Thos. Lewis photograph.

10. In 1880 the area of the station was doubled by building further platforms on the southern side of Great Queen Street. That street then became an access to both halves of the station and was known as Queens Drive.

11. Midland Railway locomotive 498 standing in the post-1880 southern half of the station. Postcard by W. Leslie Good of Kings Norton.

12. The whole of the Victorian hotel and station was demolished in the 1960s to provide the existing British Rail complex. This card dates from around 1903.

13. Users of the station will remember the subways connecting the platforms and the small tractors pulling a string of trolleys. They were intended for official use only, but many were the trainspotters who preferred them to the bridges! Card shows L.N.W.R. engine no. 5988 *Claughton* at New Street in March 1935, from a G.S. Lloyd photo.

14. L.N.W.R. engine no. 657 pictured on a 1923 postcard. Birmingham trainspotters will be able to recall memories of many happy hours spent at the ends of the station platforms.

ENTRANCE TO SNOW HILL STATION. BIRMINGHAM

15. Snow Hill was designed by W.G. Owen and opened in 1852 to take the Birmingham-Wolverhampton and Birmingham-Oxford routes, and later all the Great Western ones. This postcard shows the impressive station entrance about 1920.

16. The station occupied a long thin site between Livery Street and Snow Hill. The Great Western Hotel was designed by A. Chatwin and completed in 1863. 'Adco' series postcard.

17. Photographic card showing 3027 *Worcester* at Snow Hill in August 1905.

18. Fifty years later and the scene has hardly changed: but the station had only eighteen years of life left before closure and demolition took place. Passenger trains ceased on March 6th 1972.

19. The Grand Junction Railway was the first line into Birmingham, opening in 1837. Suburban stations were opened later, including **Great Barr** in 1862. By 1910, sixteen passenger trains stopped at this station in each direction, with five on Sundays. The journey to New Street took 18 minutes, to Walsall 15 minutes. Great Barr is no longer open. This postcard was published by Frank Nightingale.

20. London Midland & Scottish Railway engine no. 710 passing through Great Barr in 1924. The L.M.S. replaced the L.N.W.R., who had acquired the line in the 1880s.

21. When the Birmingham-Wolverhampton-Dudley line was opened in 1854, there were three stations within the modern city: Hockley, Winson Green and Handsworth. This card shows a goods train passing Handsworth Junction Box about 1930.

22. The bridge over Bournville Lane carried both the canal and the Midland line from Birmingham to King's Norton. Card posted to Ten Acre Street in November 1909.

23. King's Heath station on the Birmingham-Gloucester line was opened in 1840, closed to passengers in January 1941 and to goods in May 1966. Sixteen stopping trains (four on Sundays) in each direction were accommodated in 1910. Postcard published in the 'Clarence' series by Edwards & Co. of New Street.

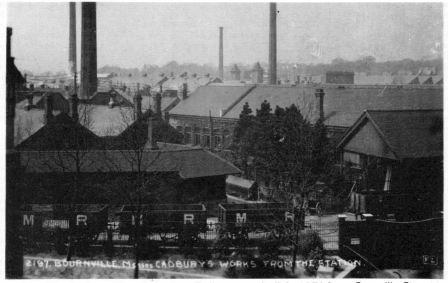

24. The Birmingham West Suburban Railway was built in 1876 from Granville Street to the Birmingham-Gloucester line at Kings Norton, with an extension connecting Granville Street to New Street. This card showing the view of Cadbury's works from the railway station at Bournville was published by T. Ryberg of Edgbaston, and posted to Bromyard in May 1913.

25. 'Stirchley Street' station was opened in 1876 but renamed **Bournville** in 1880. Card published by Austin Bros.

26. Hagley Road station was opened on the Harborne line in 1874, and became part of the London & North Western Railway, which in its turn became part of the L.M.S. system. The four-mile branch was busy in Edwardian days but was closed to passengers in November 1934. Goods traffic survived at Hagley Road for another 29 years.

Stechford Station.

27. **Stechford** on the London-Birmingham line was one of the earliest suburban stations, opened in 1844, only six years after the opening of the line: Glover of Stechford published this card c.1910.

28. **Gravelly Hill,** on the very busy Birmingham-Sutton Coldfield route, opened in 1859, owned by the London & North Western in Edwardian days. Card published by R. Benton of Erdington.

29. The Birmingham-Gloucester Railway became par
Brighton Road station was opened in 1875 and close

dland which in its turn was swallowed up by the L.M.S. y 1941. Note the boarded, rather than stone, platform.

30. Erdington station in 1908. Signs indicate where to wait for first and third class carriages.

31. The Midland line from Castle Bromwich to Walsall aroused opposition as it ran through Sutton Park. The line was opened to passenger traffic in 1879, and **Penns** station, seen here on a c.1920 card published by E.A. Butler of Walmley, closed in 1965.

32. Tyseley station on the Great Western line south to Leamington and Stratford, with a railcar at the platform. The station was opened in 1906, principally because it was at the junction of the new Stratford branch. Three years later it had an extremely busy service, with 55 weekday and 14 Sunday trains in each direction.

33. The North Warwickshire line was the last to be opened in Birmingham. In the background can be seen the construction of the embankment through Sarehole in 1906. Card by H. Munro of Birmingham.

34. Station staff at **Hall Green** about 1920.

35. Hall Green on a Geo. E. Lewis postcard, posted to Bordesley Green in July 1910. *"I am coming down tomorrow, all being well, about dinner time. Please don't forget you owe me two postcards."* Goods traffic ceased here in May 1968.

36. Though originally promoted by the Birmingham, North Warwickshire and Stratford-on-Avon Railway Company and authorised by Act of Parliament in 1984, the G.W.R. took over the enterprise. The line was opened for goods traffic in 1907 and passengers in 1908. Two years later 23 passenger trains in each direction stopped at Hall Green on weekdays, and five on Sundays.

37. The two cards on this page show off the superb array of massed flowers and hanging baskets on Hall Green station in the 1920s. Doubtless the stationmaster and 14 staff seen on illus. 34 had the time to maintain the station's immaculate appearance.

38. Yardley Wood opened for passengers in 1908. This view was apparently taken before the station was in use.

39. A crowded **Acocks Green** station in 1905 on a photographic card by Geo. E. Lewis.

40. **Olton,** one stop further down the G.W.R. line to Leamington.

41. **Moseley** station on the Birmingham-Gloucester line opened in 1867 and closed in 1941. This 1908 view shows a train approaching. Note the advert for Cotterell's Stores, Moseley, on the left.

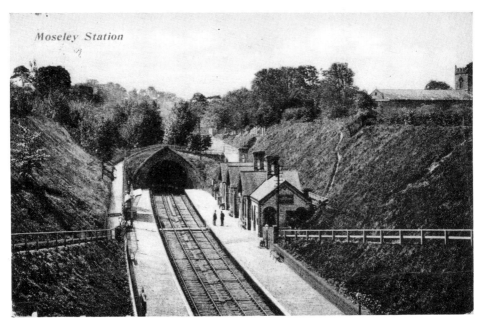

Moseley Station

42. A view of Moseley looking in the opposite direction. This and Gravelly Hill appeared on more postcards than any of the other suburban stations. Card posted at Birmingham in September 1905.

FOR AULD LANGSYNE

NORTHFIELD RAILWAY STATION

43. Northfield, on the Birmingham-Gloucester line, was still only a small village in 1869 when the station was first used. This photographic card dates from around 1912, and has been overprinted with New Year greetings.

44. Another view of Northfield, on a card published there by J.J. Davis and posted to Worcester in November 1905. Services ran from here to Redditch, Halesowen, Birmingham and Droitwich/Worcester.

45. Kings Norton was 1¼ miles north on the same line. This card by F. Willcocks features a photo taken from the footbridge. Postcard sent to Ledbury in December 1907.

46. Kings Norton was opened in 1849, nine years after the Birmingham-Gloucester line came into use. Note the huge number of adverts on the station buildings, both for railway excursions and other products.

ATION. KINGS NORTON.

47. A new footbridge was installed at Kings Norton in 1926. This card features L.M.S. engine 4040 with the travelling crane lifting it into position.

48. L.M.S. locomotive 768 at Kings Norton in May 1913.

49. Hazelwell was a late addition to the same line. Situated ³/₄ mile south of Kings Heath, it never really justified its existence. Opened in 1903, it was closed 38 years later.

Reconstruction of Aston Bridge Sunday March 25'06

A Great Engineering Feat.

This Bridge, weighing 300 tons, was placed in position in 15½ minutes.

50. Aston Bridge, carrying the L.N.W.R. line from Birmingham to Sutton Coldfield, was replaced in 1906. On Sunday 25th March of that year, the new bridge was placed in position in just 15¹/₂ minutes.

FRANKLEY VIADUCT

51. The Halesowen Joint Midland and Great Western Railway was opened in 1884, connecting Halesowen and Kings Norton. In 1902 sidings were added at Rubery, and the Rubery-Frankley line carried sand and stone for the construction of Frankley and Bartley Green reservoirs.

52. The Birmingham-Gloucester Railway ran through a tunnel at Cofton, but this was dismantled and the track widened in 1928-9, as seen on this card published by W. Leslie Good of Kings Norton.

53. A card designed by Scottish postcard artist Cynicus and published by his own company. It was overprinted with a huge number of place names, in this case Perry Barr. The card was posted at Handsworth in July 1908.

54. Perry Barr and Vauxhall stations were the only suburban stops on the Grand Junction Railway when it opened in 1837. When this card was published around 1910, eleven trains stopped in each direction on weekdays. Last train home from Birmingham was 11.05, reaching Perry Barr at 11.19 p.m.

55. Saltley repair shops in 1908. Locomotive nearest the camera, no.97, has a notice *"not to be moved"* – unlikely in the circumstances.

56. An advertising card of c.1907 vintage for the Midland Railway carriage and wagon works, Lander Street, Saltley. This oil tank wagon was built for the Indian Railways.

LONDON AND NORTH  ERN RAILWAY COMPANY.

POST CARD

THE
L & N. W. R.
SOCIETIES
OF
PICTORIAL

GOODS CLERICAL BENEVOLENT SOCIETIES

Have much pleasure in announcing the

FOURTH ANNUAL POPULAR CONCERT,

Which will be held in the

TOWN HALL, BIRMINGHAM, On *Saturday, November 16th, 1907,*

ARTISTES—

Miss ISABEL SPENCER,
(Soprano) of Principal London and Provincial Concerts.

Madame MARGUERITE GELL,
(Contralto) The Popular Birmingham Favourite.

Mr. SAMUEL MASTERS,
(Tenor) of the Royal Albert Hall, Queen's Hall,
Crystal Palace, &c., &c., Concerts.

Mr. CUTHBERT ALLAN,
(Baritone) of the Principal London and Provincial
Concerts.

Mr. WILSON JAMES (The Popular London Humourist).

Mr. GEORGE ATKINSON (Solo Pianist and Accompanist).

The St. CHAD'S QUARTETTE.

DOORS OPEN AT 7.0 P.M. - - - TO COMMENCE AT 7.45 P.M.

TICKETS, 2/- (numbered reserved); 1/- and 6d. each; and may be obtained from the Goods Offices at
CURZON STREET, MONUMENT LANE, and ASTON.

57. These cards were not only sold to the public but were used for official correspondence and advertising, as this and the next three examples show. The L.N.W.R. was the most adept of all the railway companies at using cards for publicity. The picture on the front of this featured a sleeping compartment in the royal train.

POST CARD.

L. & N. W
SERIES

For Postage in the United Kingdom only
This Space may be used for Correspondence.

(For Address Only.)

Dec. 1905.

CALENDAR, 1908.

JANUARY.	FEBRUARY.	MARCH.	APRIL.
S M T W T F S	S M T W T F S	S M T W T F S	S M T W T F S

MAY.	JUNE.	JULY.	AUGUST.
S M T W T F S	S M T W T F S	S M T W T F S	S M T W T F S

SEPTEMBER.	OCTOBER.	NOVEMBER.	DECEMBER.
S M T W T F S	S M T W T F S	S M T W T F S	S M T W T F S

The London & North Western
Railway Company

collect and deliver Goods by their own
Vans in BIRMINGHAM, and have . .

Express Goods Trains Daily

for all parts of

ENGLAND, SCOTLAND,
IRELAND, and WALES.

At their CURZON STREET, ASTON,
and MONUMENT LANE STATIONS they
have every convenience for dealing with all
kinds of GOODS and MINERALS.

At CURZON STREET they have also
A Commodious Bonded Warehouse, and
Large Cattle Docks adjoining Public Market.

58. L.N.W.R. calendar card with additional advertising, published about 1904.

**Designed and Published by
Reflections of a Bygone Age
Keyworth, Nottingham
1993**

Revised edition March 1999

**Printed by
Adlard Print and Typesetting Services,
Ruddington, Notts.**